PEEKING
UNDERGROUND

by Karen Latchana Kenney

illustrated by Steven Wood

PICTURE WINDOW BOOKS
a capstone imprint

Take a look around the park.

What do you see?

People walk and play.

Animals crawl, hop, and jump.

Plants stretch toward the sun.

Life is busy ABOVE ground.
What happens BELOW?
Flip the page to peek beneath ...

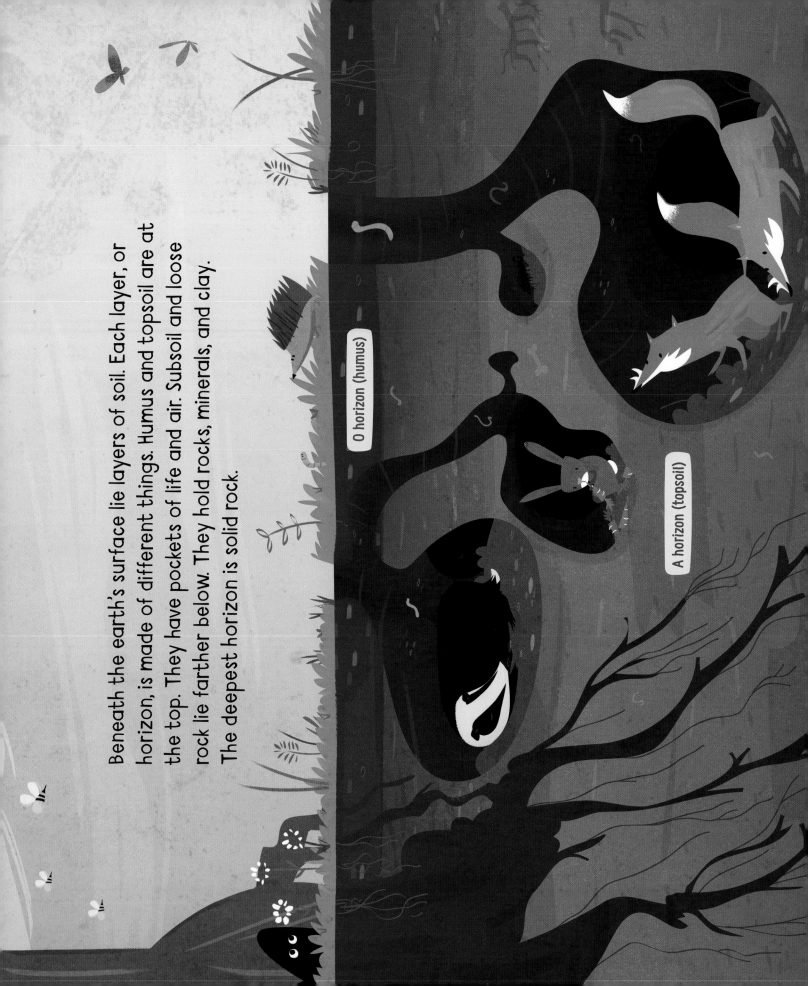

Beneath the earth's surface lie layers of soil. Each layer, or horizon, is made of different things. Humus and topsoil are at the top. They have pockets of life and air. Subsoil and loose rock lie farther below. They hold rocks, minerals, and clay. The deepest horizon is solid rock.

O horizon (humus)

A horizon (topsoil)

B horizon (subsoil)

C horizon (loose rock)

R horizon (bedrock)

The horizons formed over millions of years. Wind and sun beat down on Earth's surface. Water flowed, froze, and flowed again. Rocks, plants, and animal remains broke down into smaller and smaller pieces. The new soil settled into layers.

Right on Top

Humus is the dark, moist top layer of soil. It's made from dead plants and animals. The remains break down into nutrients. Humus is crumbly and light. Air and water pass easily through it.

earthworm

mushroom

See the mushrooms? The earthworms?
Humus supplies mushrooms and earthworms
with food. When earthworms wiggle through
the soil, they mix it. Worm droppings feed plants.

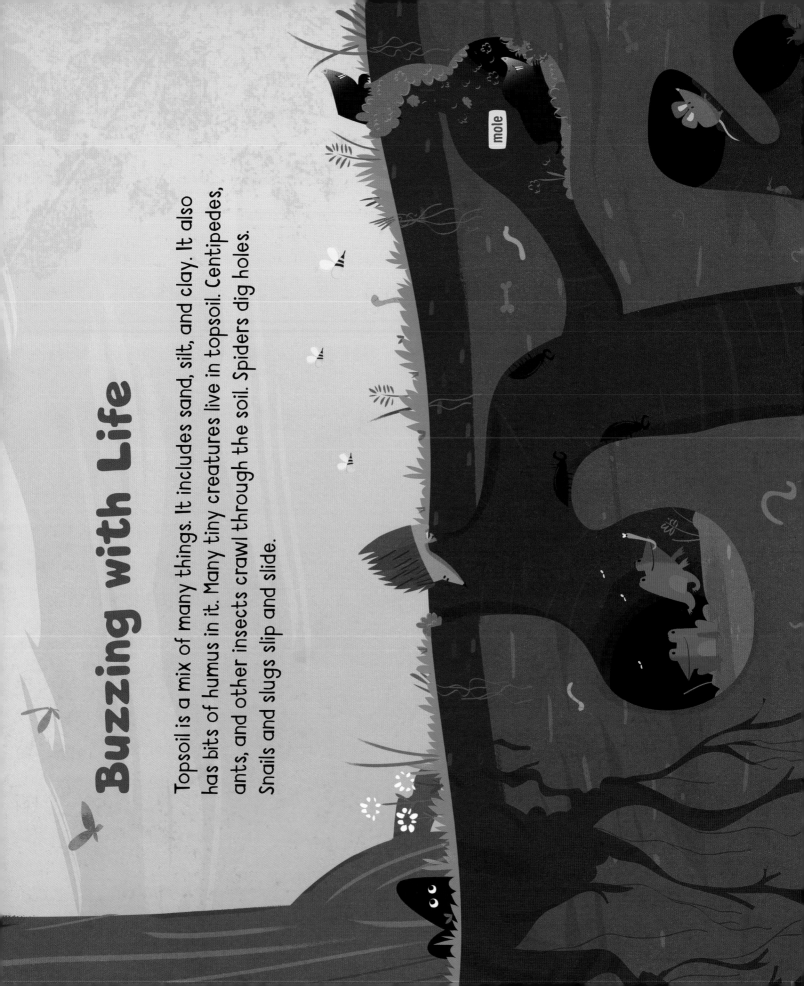

Buzzing with Life

Topsoil is a mix of many things. It includes sand, silt, and clay. It also has bits of humus in it. Many tiny creatures live in topsoil. Centipedes, ants, and other insects crawl through the soil. Spiders dig holes. Snails and slugs slip and slide.

mole

DID YOU KNOW?

Many kinds of bacteria live in topsoil. You can't see them with the naked eye. They're too tiny. Just 1 teaspoon (5 milliliters) of soil can hold close to 1 billion bacteria!

rabbit

fox

badger

Larger animals make burrows in the topsoil. Moles dig tunnels. So do rabbits and badgers. Foxes sometimes live underground too.

Plant Roots

What else lies in topsoil? Plant and tree roots! Look just below the stems on this page. See the carrots? Carrots are long, thick roots called taproots. Smaller roots branch off of them.

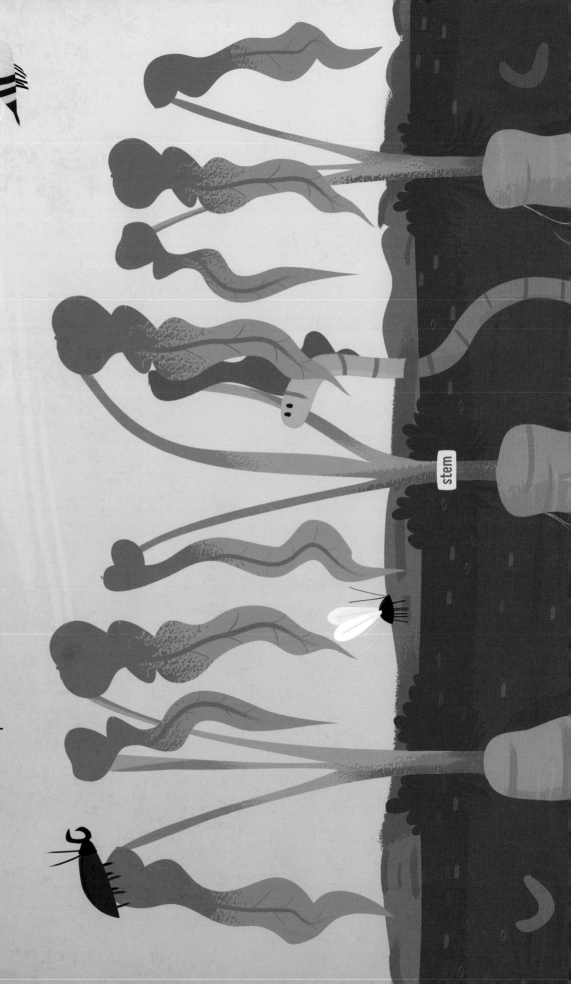

stem

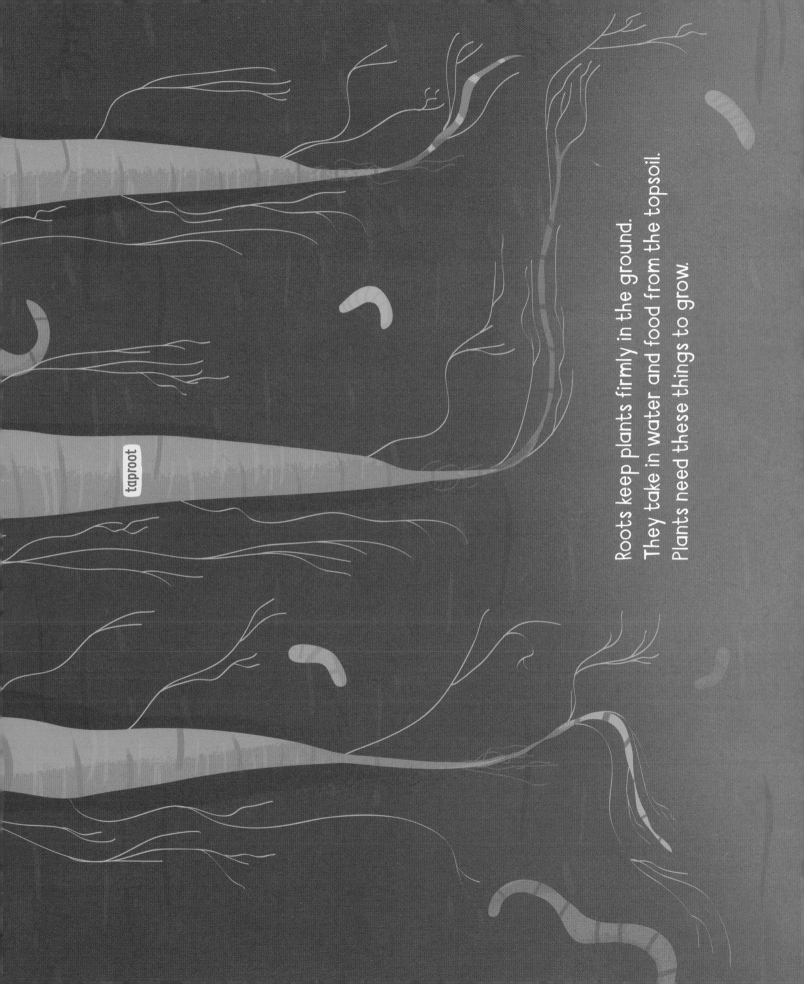

Roots keep plants firmly in the ground.
They take in water and food from the topsoil.
Plants need these things to grow.

taproot

Changing Color

Dig deeper and you'll find subsoil. See the change in color? The thick subsoil layer is much lighter than topsoil. It may be gray, tan, or even red. Subsoil is made of fine rock and clay. It has tiny amounts of metal in it.

topsoil

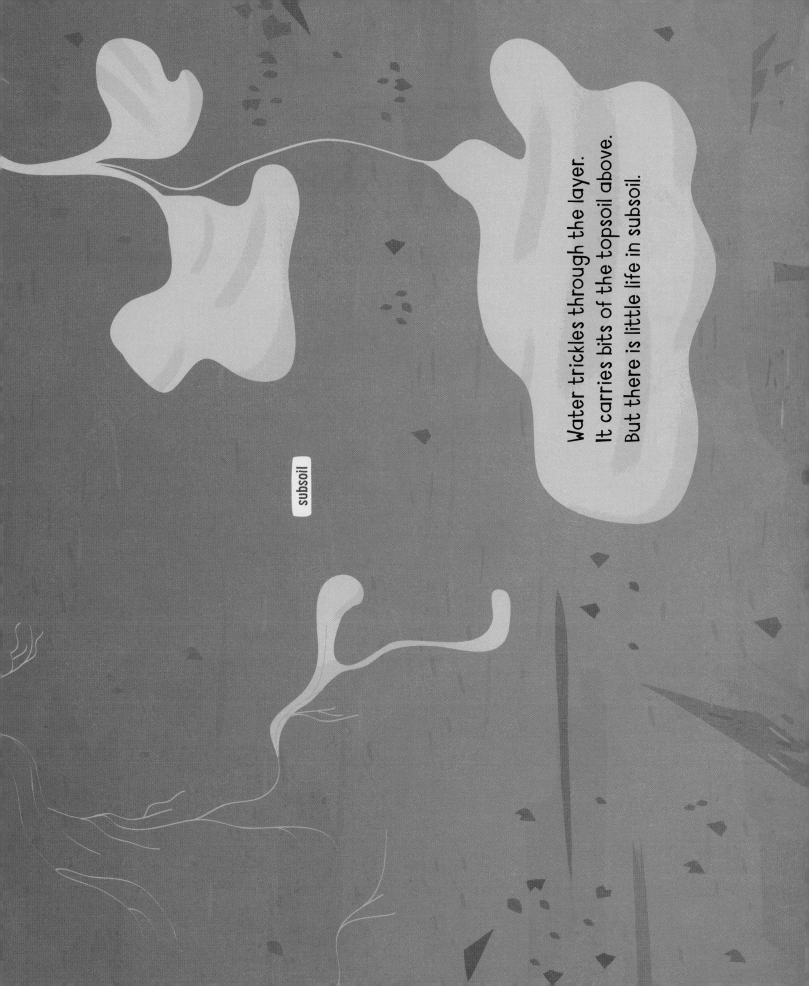

subsoil

Water trickles through the layer.
It carries bits of the topsoil above.
But there is little life in subsoil.

Follow the Water

Water collects above ground in rivers and lakes.
But it also collects underground.

lake

river

spring

sea

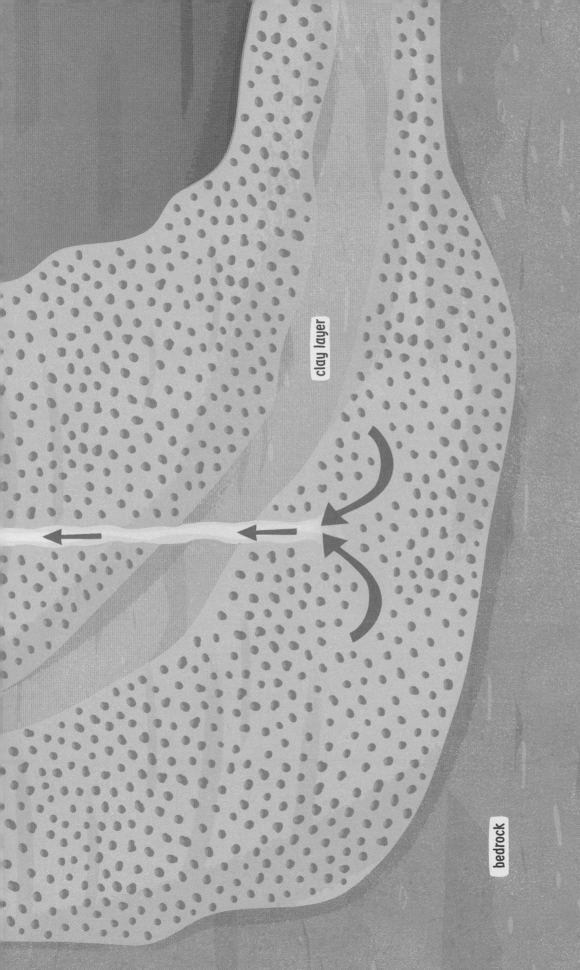

clay layer

bedrock

Water is always moving underground. Rain falls from the sky. It seeps into the soil. Gravity pulls it downward. Rock takes out much of the bacteria and dirt from the moving water. The water collects in a layer of rock. Some water leaves the rock layer through a spring.

Simply Rock

Rock, rock, and more rock! Loose, broken rocks mix with soil just below the subsoil. This layer has minerals such as quartz and mica in it. It rests on top of solid rock. Bedrock is a very deep layer. It sits at the bottom edge of Earth's crust.

loose rock

Bedrock can be many thousands of feet thick. It's often 10 to 100 times thicker than the loose rock layer above it.

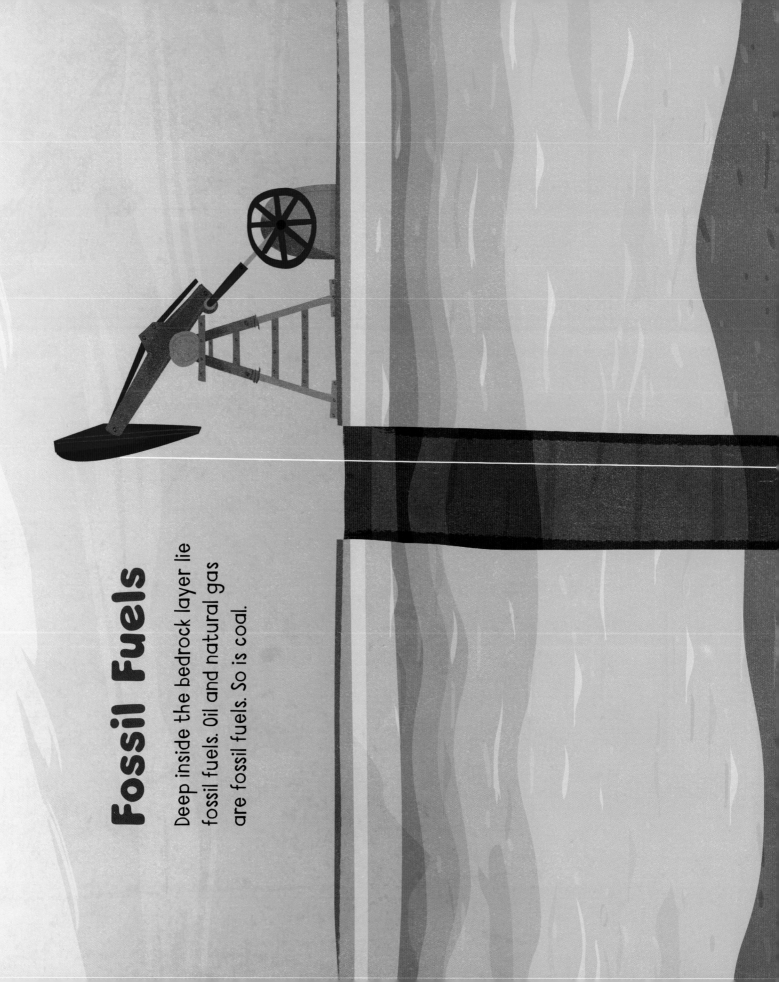

Fossil Fuels

Deep inside the bedrock layer lie fossil fuels. Oil and natural gas are fossil fuels. So is coal.

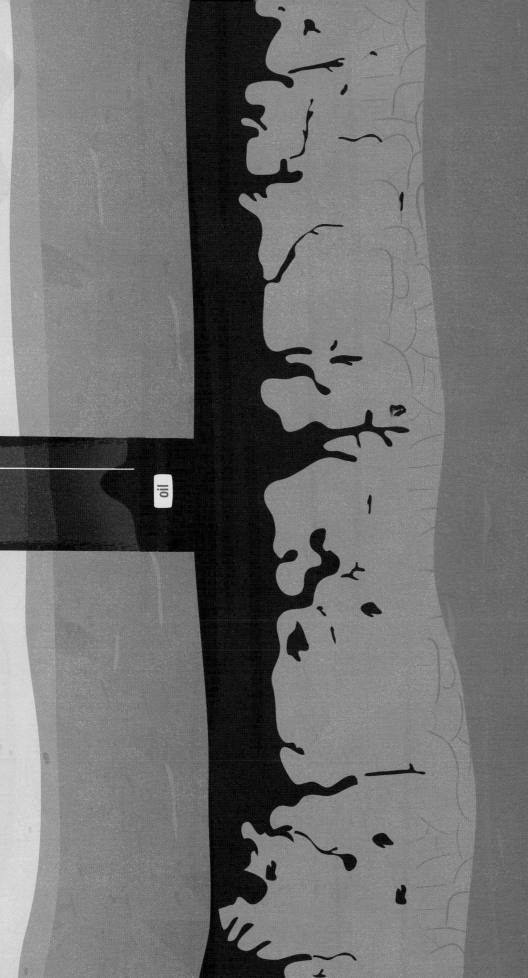

Fossil fuels formed from plants and animals that died long ago. Sand and mud covered the remains over millions of years. The remains sank deeper and deeper into the earth. The weight of the soil and rock on top of them pushed down hard. The pressure and heat turned the remains into fossil fuels.

On the Move

Earth's crust is not one piece. It is made of seven major plates. See where the two plates below meet? That line is called a fault line.

Ocean crust is heavy. It slides under the land's crust. The two crusts rub together. Sometimes they get stuck. Earthquakes happen when the crusts break free of each other.

continental plate

volcano

fault line

oceanic plate

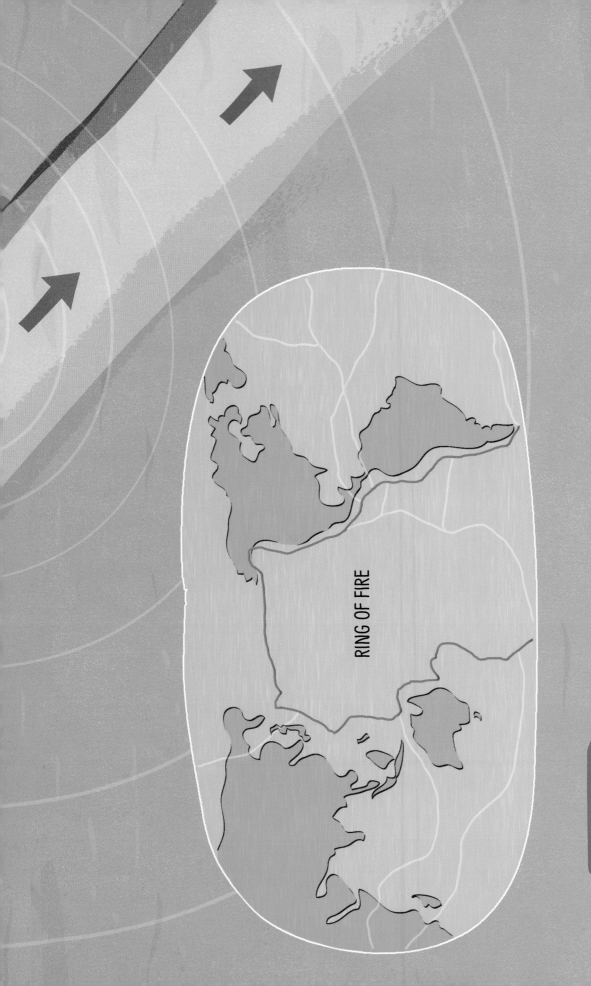

RING OF FIRE

Volcano Blast

What a sight! It's a volcano!

ash

vent

lava

side vent

Take a look inside. See the vent? It is a crack in Earth's crust. Side vents branch off of it. Hot, gooey molten rock called magma is pushed up the vents. The volcano erupts! Lava shoots out. Some cools in the air and becomes ash.

magma

Below the Crust

How far down can we go? The mantle is just below Earth's crust. It is Earth's thickest layer. The mantle is 1,800 miles (2,900 kilometers) thick. It is made up of solid and molten rock.

crust

mantle

DID YOU KNOW?

People cannot see below Earth's crust. No machine has gone deep enough to reach the mantle. Scientists make good guesses about what it's like. Much information comes from studying earthquakes. Earthquakes give off waves of energy. These waves tell scientists where and how thick Earth's layers are.

To the Core

Welcome to the center of our planet! See the outer core and the inner core? The outer core is mostly liquid metal. It is 1,400 miles (2,250 km) thick. Movement inside the outer core makes Earth a giant magnet. Earth's poles are on opposite sides of the magnet.

The inner core looks like a ball. It's the hottest part of our planet. It is 750 miles (1,200 km) thick.

NORTH POLE

crust

mantle

outer core

inner core

SOUTH POLE

Back above ground, bees buzz. Squirrels scurry into the trees. Birds pull earthworms from the soil. The grass tickles your toes. Earth is an amazing place, above the surface or underground!

GLOSSARY

bacteria—very small living things that exist everywhere in nature

bedrock—a layer of solid rock beneath the layers of soil and loose gravel

continental—having to do with Earth's land masses

fossil fuel—a natural fuel formed from the remains of plants and animals; coal, oil, and natural gas are fossil fuels

gravity—an invisible force that pulls objects toward Earth's core

humus—the wet, dark part of soil that is made of rotted plants and animals

lava—the hot, liquid rock that pours out of a volcano when it erupts

magma—molten rock found deep inside Earth

magnet—a piece of metal that attracts iron or steel: a magnet has two ends called poles

mantle—a thick layer of hot rock between Earth's crust and core

mineral—a solid found in nature that has a crystal structure

molten—melted by heat

nutrient—a part of food, like a vitamin, that is used for growth

oceanic—having to do with the ocean

pressure—a force made by pressing on something

silt—small grains that are smaller than sand and larger than clay; silt is made up of tiny bits of rock

spring—a source of water that comes from the ground

subsoil—the layer of Earth between topsoil and loose rock

taproot—the main root of certain plants, such as a carrot

topsoil—the top layer of soil that is rich with humus

CRITICAL THINKING USING THE COMMON CORE

1. Why do plants and animals live in the humus and topsoil layers? (Key Ideas and Details)

2. Explain how fossil fuels form. (Key Ideas and Details)

3. Why do you think it's so difficult to explore beneath Earth's crust? (Integration of Knowledge and Ideas)

READ MORE

Oxlade, Chris. *Volcanoes.* Learning About Landforms. Chicago: Heinemann Library, 2014.

Taylor-Butler, Christine. *Experiments with Soil.* My Science Investigations. Chicago: Heinemann Library, 2012.

Walker, Sally M. *Studying Soil.* Do You Dig Earth Science? Minneapolis: Lerner, 2013.

INTERNET SITES

FactHound offers a safe, fun way to find Internet sites related to this book. All of the sites on FactHound have been researched by our staff.

Here's all you do:

Visit *www.facthound.com*

Type in this code: 9781479586660

Check out projects, games and lots more at
www.capstonekids.com

Special thanks to our adviser, Bryce Hoppie, PhD, PG, Professor of Geology, Minnesota State University, Mankato, for his expertise.

Picture Window Books are published by Capstone,
1710 Roe Crest Drive, North Mankato, Minnesota 56003
www.mycapstone.com

Library of Congress Cataloging-in-Publication Data
Cataloging-in-publication information is on file with the
Library of Congress.
ISBN 978-1-4795-8666-0 (library binding)
ISBN 978-1-4795-8670-7 (paperback)
ISBN 978-1-4795-8674-5 (eBook PDF)

Editor: Jill Kalz
Designer: Russell Griesmer
Creative Director: Nathan Gassman
Production Specialist: Katy LaVigne
The illustrations in this book were created digitally.

Printed and bound in US
007536CGS16

LOOK FOR ALL THE BOOKS IN THE SERIES:

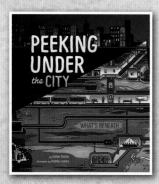

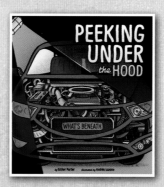